Dark Horses and Little Turtles

and Other Poems from the Anthropocene

Richard Stephen Felger

Polytropos Press

Tucson   2020

Dark Horses and Little Turtles

ISBN 978-0-9843892-1-6

Polytropos Press

www.polytropos.com

Edited and designed by Gregory McNamee

at Rancho Lagarto, Tucson, Arizona

in the COVID summer of 2020

Contents

It is now beyond all reasonable doubt that birds evolved from little turtles. While certain biosystematic positions and sequences are yet to be worked out, the recent discovery of the flying feathered-turtle (upper right) and the featherless bird-turtle (left center) are major breakthroughs in chelonian-avian phylogeny studies. Furthermore, we can now assume that gorphomorphs (lower left), smiling scowl-scats (bottom center), mermaids (right center), and the salamander-smile syndrome (bottom right) have likewise evolved from proto-chelonian stocks. (See McClure and Janie, "Model Theories for the Evolution of the Universe," manuscript in disintegration.)

Dark Purple

The osprey
    lifts the gray morning
off a huge *cardón*
    from her giant nest of sticks
sand and the smell of broom
night's last bat

tamarisk wet in the wind
skinny dogs and a brown pig
gobbling grouper guts on the tide flat
       rippled and silvery as the sky turns
gooseneck barnacles
sea slugs snuggled in the wet
      sand-cast egg case
of the snail of the moon
flaccid seaweeds
      and green eelgrass

turtle shells dance on abandoned *jacáles*
the wind
it is almost February
adobe crumbling on mainstreet
nomadic people
    settled in plastitrash

digging for clams
      donde corre el corriente
thousands of dark purple sand dollars
rise from darkness
as the tide creeps across the empty lagoon
      at sunset

Little Turtles

The mist clears.
fleshy fields of yellow leaves
surround
steely desert ferns

the Sun rises
with you with me

The mist clears.
little turtles pour out of the sand
beckoned to the sea
by brightness
they disappear
in swampy mangrove root refuge
fiddler crabs scuttle sideways
across manta-ray holes
in the lagoon
drained by the moon

Gorgonian corals.
sand dollars
touched by red tide
and sponges like soft brain coral
bleach brittle
at the abandoned fish camp
flat turtle barnacles
like empty eyes from the sea
staring out at the desert

Pinacateño

Pinacateño
Pinacateño
Pinacateño
Pinacateño

the wind, the wind
amaranths in the wind

tops blowing off the dunes
just after the rain
high lava snow
goes quick
ocotillo wavering
In a tiny desert-pavement pool

the Goddess of Sandfood
with the God of Water
dusty breasts
deep-water tinaja
the wind, the wind
tumbleweed riding the dunes
seeding

precise antelope tracks
and the color of clay pottery

coyotes yelling at dawn in the cloudless sky
saguaros sway in the wind

pray for rain
pray for sandfood

Pinacateño
Pinacateño
Pinacateño
Pinacateño

Requiem
for the Desert
by the Harnessing of Solar Energy

listen to the sun
dance on the dunes
smoothed sands watered green

tell the children, once upon a time
drifting dunes
over the Buried Range
evening primroses
opening perfume
white
for the sphinx moth
distant dust
stirring
specks of antelope
the Sierra San Pedro Mártir
a hundred miles
ragged in the red sunset
on the way
to the land of the dead

Song of a Long Journey through Turtle Island

we move from valley to valley
a generation or two at a time

each valley
has new plants
and sometimes a new animal
now we have spread to the end of the land

I
she thinks it's brave
making love
in the grass
grown tall
since spring migration

a whole valley beyond
and there's nobody there

growl
saber-toothed cat
rake
soft gore
from your
rotting mastodon

condors
fall from the sky

dire wolves
wait in the shadow

I keep thinking of the valley beyond
fire the forest
burn the darkness
let the sun
touch the ground

summery grass
greens the valley
bison
elk   antelope
and camelops
come to graze

sing for the valley
sing for the sun and fire

I sat by the knees
    of elders
now I teach
    our songs

make no mistakes
and there will always be sun
    and fire

we move
with the herds
sweet biscuit roots
and acorns

nights are dry
and easy
on animal skins
made soft
with oak bark
and buffalo brains
brush shelters

woven into the land
fine as a weaver's nest

all paths
turn to water

we camp so carefully
you would never know
        we were there
no place
    shall stink our stink

we quarrel when
    there are too many
and move on
rather than change our ways
as long as there are valleys

II

ice
grinds into the sea
across the continent
for a hundred centuries
there is no passage
        in the west

the beach wanders out
century by century we live
where the sea
will someday return

funny little people
in furs
trickle down the east side
in skin boats

birch and larch
spruce and dark horses
wait in the melt
inch by inch
until there is passage
       all the way north

people speaking a whole new language
are pouring in
ten or twenty or so
       every year

faces too wide
women too fat
but fine long and shining black hair
and seem as smart as us
although they are crude

they kill
with fearsome long weapons
tipped in hard stone
       made sharp-edged
like some hard-on
       with a stone foreskin

we are quick
to make those fine things

III

not so many big animals
children just play in the weeds

we sing
of giant jaguars
            turning real
in the cooling embers

time changes so much
I hardly know who I am anymore

where did all these people come from?

clinging to the earth
with possessions
status   slaves
            and war

we are free
only in the ragged lands
away from the valley

the valley
overrun with farmers
wounding the earth to grow plants
hoarding food
        in dark stinking square houses
                in gourd-shaped things made from cooked dirt

The deer and puma and mastodon
            are gone from the valley

some say to raid
and not kill
because they are brothers
and mothers

staying in the same place
looking at the same things.   puke!
feeding old people
imagine wanting to live too old
to run and hunt and make love

I wonder if their dead
are the ghosts
of those wild nights
when there is no moon

stay behind
with your dog
food and water enough
to prepare
for the Long Journey

IV

the Great Drought is coming
nobody cares except my shaman friend

says there's nothing she can do about it anyway
the People have always lived here
and
everywhere else
has someone

I feel like the day
we marched on the Pentagon

so I left Arizona one fine spring in 1272
and wandered north
where there once was a great shield of ice
so long ago

Biomass Balance

we displace other animals
this planet of whales and people
supports only so much
about ten times more green than animal
    250 million at Christ time
now 4,000 million*
    250 million more every 3.5 years

well it seems to balance
all the animals gone since we came along
blue whales took a lot of the slack
but great whales are nearly gone
and soon more than half
the animals of the earth
will be gone
forever

* That was 1974. This is 2020.
no surprise, but who would have believed
7.8 billion heading for 8?

THE TURTLOID PLAN*

You always need a plan, for you and for me, and for your government, and for our prison warden. Subcomandante Pichiquate recommends this one to show how governments should operate, with the notable exceptions of DungaStan, Italy, and the Falkland Islands. Furthermore, you can't rely on rain from the weather coyote; she fibs like a politician who has not followed the Turtloid Plan. But not to worry, the great mossy mata-mata from the brown ooze will make everything right, just like it used to be when caviar flowed for the righteous. And great white rhinoceroses will walk again.

The Last Turtle

The events recorded below took place in heaven in a subdivision reserved for extinct and soon to be extinct species.

In order of their appearance, the informants are:

Hank, a giant land tortoise weighing 290 pounds, with an elegant shell 4.8 feet in length. His species was autochthonous to the oak-grasslands of Texas and northern Mexico. Each segment or shield of his carapace has a star pattern—yellow rays on a dark shell—on the order of the Madagascar star tortoise. He has a pointed blond beard.

Parveen, a Persian leopard, has long eyelashes and luscious legs. She is an experienced predator.

Ondine is a large Atlantic leatherback turtle. She is extraordinarily well developed, sort of a chelonian Brunhilde. Her carapace is patent leather with the characteristic seven ridges (*siete filos*) of the leatherback. Her plastron is loose-weave pale yellow knit, and the five ridges indicated with black straps at strategic points and a wide black zipper down the middle.

Members of various other extinct and nearly extinct higher vertebrates come and go, e.g., imperial woodpecker, saber-toothed cat, some people in a Cadillac convertible, pygmy mammoth, California condor, and Steller's sea cow.

Act I

[Late afternoon in front of Pleistocene House, a Hollywood-style apartment —thin stucco walls, swimming pool in the middle and some smoggy tropical-looking plants. Sign in front advertises "Pleistocene House: . . . Heaven's most exclusive address . . . luxurious condominium living for the extinct or soon to be," and in much smaller print, "Higher vertebrates only."]

HANK: [*walking slowly on stage, plops down near Parveen, gets up, turns his head toward her, stretching his neck out in the manner of a giant tortoise*] What are you doing here?

PARVEEN: A man did it. He wanted my skin.

HANK: Let's rub shells.

PARVEEN: Shove off, you dirty old chauvinistic turtle.

HANK: Let's rub shells.

PARVEEN: You haven't even got any teeth.

HANK: I have a big pink tongue and a wet mouth.

PARVEEN: Your sister lays eggs.

HANK: Not anymore.

PARVEEN: Will you buy me an apartment?

HANK: I don't need one.

PARVEEN: You will when it gets cold.

HANK: Let's rub shells.

PARVEEN: You'll get lethargic when the sun goes down and the night cools off.

HANK: Not if you'll buy me an apartment.

PARVEEN: Hey, what are you doing here? This is a restricted neighborhood.

HANK: We came here with the first Indians.

PARVEEN: Can't you read? It says "higher vertebrates only."

HANK: My uncle invented the penis.

PARVEEN: [*putting paw down Hank's pants*] Let me feel it.

HANK: AAArrgghh! Retract your claws!

PARVEEN: [*removing paw*] Yecchh, just an inverted cloaca . . . . [*strutting a bit, changing mood, she breathes deep and sexy in his face*] Will you buy me a new fur coat?

HANK: [*recoiling in disgust*] Ugh, whew . . . You need chlorophyll. You oughta go on a macrobiotic diet of organic fruit and vegetables.

PARVEEN: [*rolling big dark eyes*] I EAT MEAT!

Act II

[*Patio of Pleistocene House. Ondine swims in a little plastic pool. She splashes about daintily. There is a waterbed on the pool deck.*]

HANK: [*walking slowly on stage, as before, neck stretching, turning slowly in the manner of a giant land tortoise*] Hi, gorgeous. [*she turns her head nonchalantly toward him, but scarcely acknowledges his presence, her enormous black eyelashes remain half closed; she continues to splash about, daintily*] Let's rub shells.

ONDINE: OK, hot turtle, but first . . . you must swim . . . across the great water . . . and meet me at my island . . . by the silvery beach . . . at full moon . . . nearest the summer solstice.

HANK: How will I know how to get there?

ONDINE: The stars will show you the way to our love.

HANK: But how will I know which beach?

ONDINE: By the vibrations . . . the symphony of the waves breaking on the steep coral beach . . . waves on the reef . . . and reverberating on the great cliffs . . . surrounding the cove. No other place makes music like it.

HANK: But how can I be certain it's the right beach, or even the right island?

ONDINE: You will know.

HANK: You mean like back when we were in the egg? [*holding his body with his arms and snuggling*] When I get stoned, or sometimes just as I am dozing off, I hear that . . . well, it sort of sounds like music, strange music. I know this sounds kind of weird, but is that what you mean?

ONDINE: Yes, of course, that's it, and like before DDT, ODD, and PCB.

HANK: Oh, I don't have to know about all that sort of stuff. I came here with the first Indians.

ONDINE: I knew it was a man.

HANK: Let's ball.

ONDINE: OK, but it would be perverted without first . . . swimming across the great water . . . by the full moon nearest the summer solstice . . . to the silvery beach . . . while the tides and the waves and the sands and the coral . . . and the rocks and the cliffs play our song. Golly, you gotta know it's right.

HANK: Ahhh shit! [*walking slowly onto the waterbed, he starts bouncing up and down*]

Acts III–VI

We regret that the rest of the drama has been cancelled due to defunding of endangered species regulations.

How Things Got the Way They Are

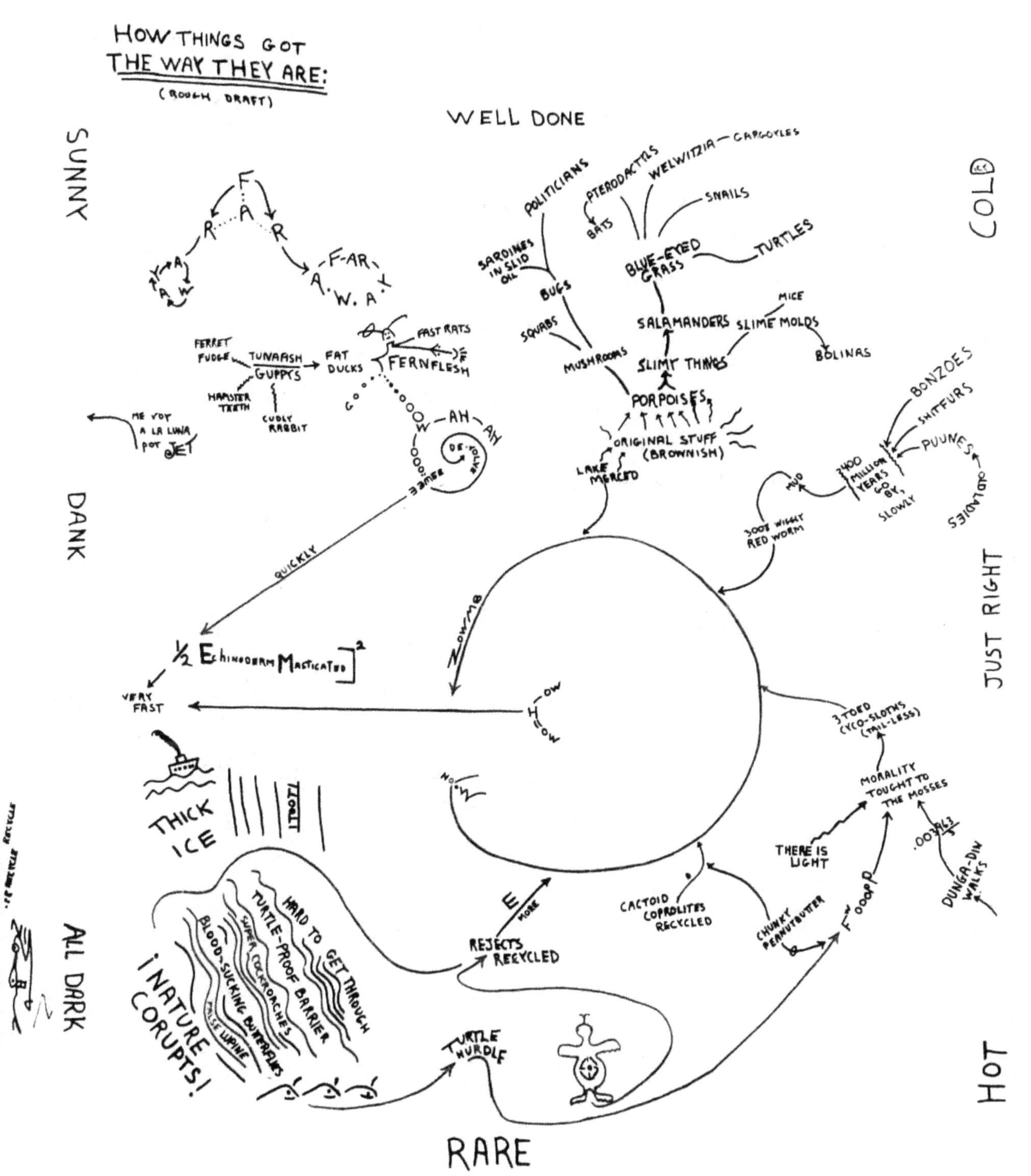

I was trying to teach a student to parrot the Krebs Cycle for a test
        but gave up on an unresponsive victim.
Why bother when you can just look up the beauty
        of that great life swirl and its tentacles.
(I hate tests and somehow managed cycling through
        pseudomagico-initiation tests called education.)

While everyone else was doing other things my mind
        drifted to fun versions of the holy cycle on scrap paper.
Ended up with the Turtloid Plan and How Things Got the Way They Are.
        A friend said you must have been stoned
        since it was Marin County in the 70s.
Not so, I was just having fun
        and I bet Krebs Cycling Nobel Prizers
        Albert Szent-Györgyi and Hans Adolf Krebs
        had their fun too,
        though I wonder about the slighted William Arthur Johnson.

Río Colorado

—for Seth

devil claws
tangle tumbleweed
rolling seed
down Black Mesa

shadows spread
from Kaiparowits

oil slicks   the San Juan
speedboats cruise Glen Canyon
at high water
30 million years
before the canyon began

pick the concrete out of the River
ride the snowmelt to the Delta

the River dreams
canyon depths

screwbean
amaranth   jojoba and chia
learn to crack
mesquite

string a double strand
of cottonwood   willow and ash
I'll show you a place with dinosaurs
There's sand in the bottom of the waterfall
There's sand in the bottom of the canyon

Dark Horses

dark horses
race the whirling
   whirlwind
      eye of the wind
         center of the nebula
           galaxy
              eye to the universe

ride into the canyon
three water ouzels
   hide and dip behind the last clear water
      ride out on the suspension bridge
         to the eye of infinity

Animals I Saw on Election Day

wasps
wait for the sun
in schisty granite

rock wrens
and a long-tail bush lizard
watch for insects
on stone walls

virgin worker wasps
come home
licking each other
for recognition

first bat
zigzags into the sky

crouching
long like a neighbor cat
the desert gray fox—dark muzzle
and black-tipped tail   whale

thick fall fur   agave
right up to the olive tree
snatched a piece of fried chicken   sea turtle
and trotted off
through paloverde and prickly pear   saguaro

22

more than animal
something closer
perhaps
I am desert gray fox

lion marmoset
and mouse lemur

aye-aye

1,000 unnamed orchids
hornbills and Hopi prophecies

Euphorbias and Passionvines

The old woman wood mask
worn in the sea
of pounding driftwood
on glacier smooth rocks.

A slender cactus slithers over the copal tree
her resin
smoldering
on cathedral steps
crosses carved on stained sabino.
The desert fern
in a mossy crotch
laced in scarlet passionvine
sing Jesuit mockery,
quetzals glitter
in the rainyellow
afternoon forest
of
emerald bees
summoned to
intoxicating deceit
by ultraviolet orchid tricks.

The girl
        in green velvet
        on a red dune
her goats graze
        the galleta
when
black horses
on the whirlwind
woven in willow splints
rode with the ghost of Geronimo.

Stretch eagle-down prayers into the rising sun.
Empty cradleboards
          of palo blanco steamed and bent
and backed in apple box boards
          bound in nylon.

Flash
the snow melting
the canyon running
flood
stirs ephemeral leaves
over ocotillo bones
dipped in blood
turning to
hummingbird flowers.

Saint George
          on a white horse
slays a green dragon
          and rescues the maiden
bound in a euphorbia tree.
The slit-eye gecko
waits beyond the sunset.

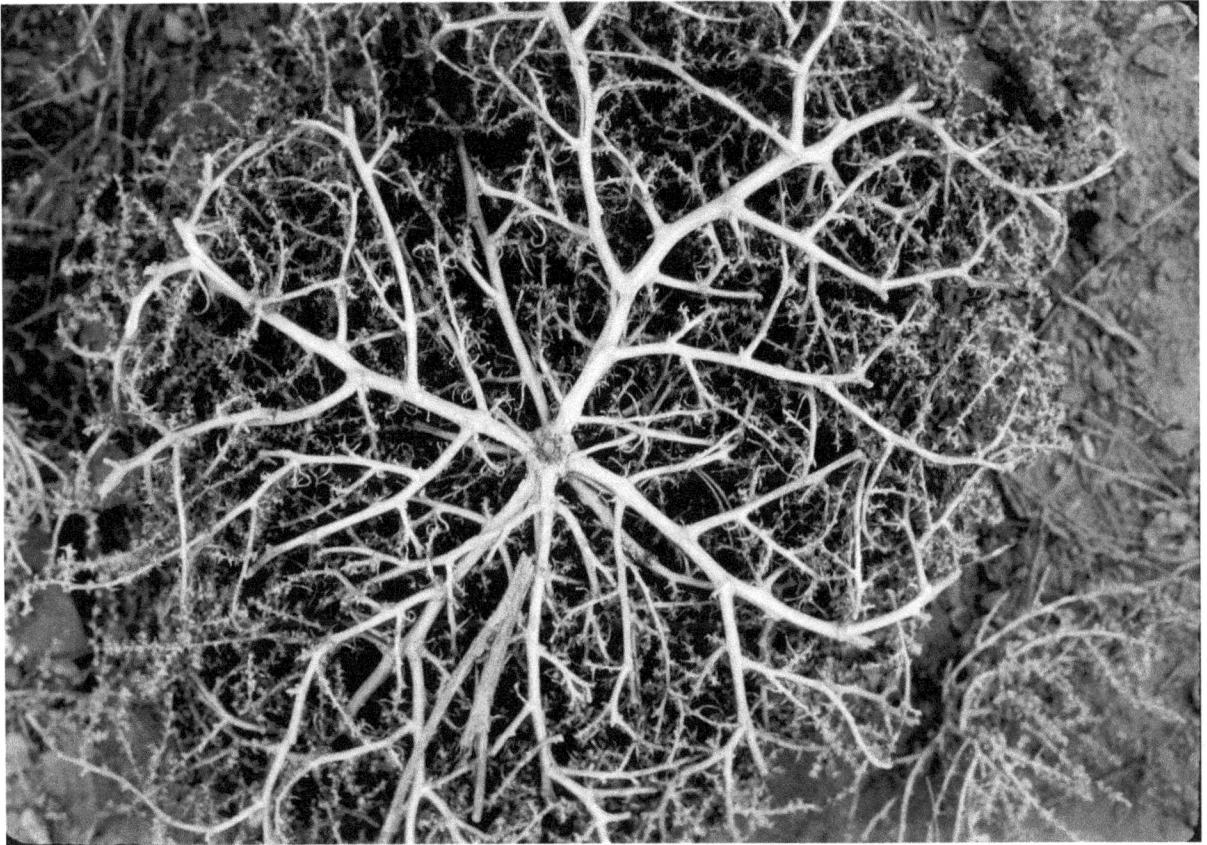

Flashflood

life flows
    continuum

now and then
        streams end
            some in resplendent swirls
      others swerve
          into vacant channels.
Suddenly
    flashing flood debris
        and muck
sucking Energy
      from the dancing waters
the human flashflood   wavecrest
     crashes
onto floodplain rocks
fresh wet earth
for sunflowers and slimemolds

Water and Food in a Dry World

No civilization
      no species lasts forever.
Come along on this illusion
      through time for food
        from this,
our upper Gila Forest Wilderness home-place
      to the Delta at River's End
and back upriver through the centuries
      making a few stops back to Gila home-place
and Food for the Future.

How many Gila Forest people 10,000 years ago?
Over 650 Gila River miles draining 60,000 square miles,
Spruce at 9,000 feet
      Flowing to the Gila/Colorado confluence at the
        heart of the Sonoran Desert
and on to River's End at the Great Delta.
How many people 10,000 years ago?
or 1,000 years ago or yesterday?
What did they eat?
How many species did you eat today?
Yesterday I did 27, half of them from two packages,
stuff native to the Old World and anywhere but here.

13,000 years ago
      all the megafauna meat we ever wanted
they weren't afraid of us
      so hunting wasn't as much fun as later millennia.
American camels, American mastodons,
      baby elephant tastes best
      easier to kill and less butcher mess
      less chance of dire wolves
        lurking in blood fragrance.
Giant tortoises, and when they were gone

we got bolson tortoises
            turn them over and put them on the fire.
Bison, horses, giant beavers, ground sloths, tapirs
            and river otters for the finest pelts.

We live on the Continental Divide
            a land of secret foods.
Every drop of river water thrusting energy eastward
            into the rising sun,
from the Mimbres toward the Atlantic.
On the other side water-drops package energy
            swirling westward from the Gila headwaters
                chasing the setting sun
                    to the Pacific side of Turtle Island
            and on to the Great Delta.
All along the Gila drainage
The People used 800 or more
            species of plants and animals for food.
Or maybe it was 1,000 or more.
We will look at a few major ones

We are all the way to River's End
churning into the sea
at the Gulf of California.
The river so wide
            you can't see the other side
Cottonwood and willow forests,
all that water, heat, and nutrients
            those trees could grow 30 feet a year.
The place teems with fish
            and big sea turtles.
And 400 more species lurk in the wet mud.
It's hot and sweaty, early afternoon,
            September 26, 1540.
Hernando de Alarcón arrives with two ships.
            The children are scared and run away.

That pair of sea monsters,
alive because we see their wings move.
       Is one a boy and the other a girl?
The shaman says
       No fear, child
       just non-round houses on huge rafts
          ' pushed by big imitation bat wings.
Hernando de Alarcón and his crew
       greet us in friendship and strange food.
We give them
       golden Nipa grain from the sea
          sun baked in mesquite flour,
dusted with cattail pollen,
dried yucca fruits,
       fresh fish and sea turtle meat
       white-seed amaranth and panic grain
fresh corn and dried squash curls.
They learn about our 30-foot tides
       when their big bat-wing rafts
          get grounded in our mud as Mother Moon
pulls the water away every day,
and then sends it roaring back on the tidal bore.

I treasured
Edward Castetter's
       accounts of Southwest food plants.
first intrigue for Nipa
perennial saltgrass, *Distichlis palmeri*
at the Colorado Delta
       washed by sea tide
dribbling down the Gulf of California
       in tidal lagoons.
Mainstay for the Cocopah People
       slapping grain heads into canoes
          or scooping it from tidal windrows.

Seawater Grain for the World
   as rising sea scorches rice bowls of the Orient.

I was privileged to be awarded funds
to search the world for salt-tolerant
   aridland food crops.
I told the kind foundation officers in New York
   "With those funds we could develop Nipa,
     a real sea-water grain."
They admonished me like talking to a child with a Ph.D.
"Everything is known about Mexico and the Southwest,
   we want you to search remote parts of the World
for new aridland/salt tolerant food plants."
And so I did.
That was long before Silke and I migrated
to the upper Gila watershed
before I learned about local Gila Forest foods
   native perennial grains
     for no-till dryland farming
to reform agriculture.

No wonder The People
   did not want to leave so sweet a place
     so much divine diversity of wild cuisine.
But I am getting ahead of the story.

Accounts from Alarcón's September
   foray to the lower Colorado and Gila rivers
tell of bringing seeds
   like wheat, and even chickens.
But those early Old World gifts did not endure.
The People only knew hot-weather crops,
   the holy trinity of Corn, Beans, and Squash,
each with a richness of variation.
I suppose The People did not know
   wheat is a cool-season grower,

for late spring harvest,
>and does survive summertime heat.

Later European incursions
>arrived with more cool-season crops:
>more wheat, barley, oats,
>carrots, lettuce, cabbage and more mustards.

Crops that do not die
>in the first or last frost.

Drive down the highway to Phoenix
imagine the Gila,
Green fields and gallery forests.
There, the Akimel O'odham, the River Pimas
farmed and feasted on fish,
one was a species of minnow that grew to six feet.
The River now as dry
as the answer Arizona kids
>give on tests, marking "river" as "dry."

Amadeo Rea tells of farms "By the River's Green Edge."
Akimel O'odham people sold surpluses
>to 49ers going to the California gold fields,

the military, or anyone else.
1922: Ashurst-Hayden Diversion Dam
>blocks the Gila River

provides irrigation for progressive Anglo farmers
>and a cheap labor force

by depriving water to Pima farmers.
So it says in the *Congressional Record*.
Get off the highway,
>And you see a dry river and dusty poverty.

Alarcón made it past Gila Bend
Where the river slices by
>the hottest driest Sonoran Desert.

Even here, or I should say, especially here
Visions of no-till desert agriculture

multicropping
        like Native gardens in the desert world.
More than 140 species,
18 percent of Sonoran Desert plant species
        provided food.
Here are a few for sustainable agriculture to fit the land:

Organpipe cactus, *Stenocereus thurberi*,
fruit to match the world's finest wine.
        Grow it on sandy raised beds
                in speckled shade of a mesquite orchard.
Grows well and fast in summer heat with a little water and
        fertilizer.
(Saguaro's fruits are good with ice cream, but they grow too
        slow)

Mesquites, *algarrobos*, *Prosopis*,
legume orchards to feed the world
Large-pod *algarrobos*, key foods in Bolivia and Peru.
        A Jesuit brought Peruvian *algarrobo* to Hawaii
                they called it *kiawe*—to sway in the ocean breeze
Honey and velvet mesquites are for the Southwest.

Foothill **paloverde**, *Parkinsonia microphylla*,
astounding yields of high-protein seeds
        a legume for extreme desert orchards.

Desert fan palm, *Washingtonia filifera*,
high harvests of small, delicious dates.
        Only needs water within 3 feet of the trunk,
and poor-quality water will do.

Desert wolfberry, *Lycium fremontii*,
a desert goji berry,
        extreme desert-hardy shrubs
major O'odham harvests in April.

Farmer, farmer, hedge your bets, intercrop, fit the crop to the land.

Click to upper Gila River home-place
you still read "they ate seeds and roots"
but Apache people knew
      more than 100 species of wild food plants
You become farmers
      when you make too many people,
and no longer roam as you please
      eating what you please.

Apache red-grass, *Zuloagaea bulbosa* (aka *Panicum bulbosum*).
They say it's the best tasting and easiest to harvest.
For no-till farming.
Perennial Gila grains, 50–70 percent higher protein than wheat.

Big sacaton, *Sporobolus wrightii*,
      as tall as a horse's belly, it's still here.
Big, tough grass, drought and salt tolerant
      high yields of grainlike flour that needs no milling.
The most immediate new major grain crop for the West and the World.

Gray oak, *Quercus grisea*,
tasty acorns
      no leaching just like the rest of our Mega-Mexico oaks.
For orchards and hedgerows.

Native mustards like **wild peppergrass**, *Lepidium thurberi*,
Not just red or green in New Mexico,
      but red, green, and white—white from peppergrass flowers
Native mustards for new chile flavors.

Wild tarragon, *Artemisia dracunculus,*
the wild North American variety,
subtle condiment,
      leafy stems tips, and seeds too.
The first Zuni food
      after emerging from the great Sipapu.

Apache food taboos include fish and waterfowl,
And you don't eat bear's food, like coffee berry.
You have to be rich to have food taboos.
Do poor people demand gluten-free bread?

I thought I was original:
      "Fit the crop to the land,
        don't change the land to fit the crop."
But J. Russell Smith said it in 1929, in
Tree Crops: A Permanent Agriculture.

Friends:
Let the Gila and the Colorado
      run all the way.
Take out their dams
      and tell the new ones to go away.
Let the rivers run
all the way to the Delta.

we walked all day
     and
the waterhole was dry

Invasion

Fernando takes me to the cave on the Hill of the Rooster where
Moctezuma and Jesus conferred. And over there, by the morning-
glory trees along the river is where Roman soldiers killed Jesus. But
"that was a thousand five hundred years before contact." He tells
me there is more than one truth.

13,000 years ago
The People follow the sea to new land
Reeds bundled and lashed together,
      paddling to mysterious sea fog islands.
Tasty tame little mammoths
      and giant sea otters for the finest pelts you will ever know.
The big animals
      are onto our ways and run away.
It was easier in the old days,
      even though it wasn't much fun
         hunting animals so stupid
            you can just walk right up and kill them.
Time to move on
      this place stinks from our refuse.
Some clan members are leaving,
      going past the misty mountains
         and we are going with them,
      even beyond the last vision quest.
Moving on for easier meat
         and getting away from old women
            telling us what to do.
We are the first people
      into this animal-filled river place.

1,000 years ago
We come into vacant land
      foolish farmers overpopulated,
         overharvested.

Cut trees until the rivers ran brown
        and then dry.
Crammed into dank dark mud rooms
        piled on top of each other
            like amplexing toads.
We are smarter, we are hunters,
        we are not buried in possessions.
Elder Old Man says possessions
        are like stink on shit
            easy to make, hard to get rid of.
We know when to move.
Our women know
        how to prevent unwanted brats.
But some things are tough.
When you are too old to keep up,
        we leave you in the desert
            with some water and a dog.

1540

Stories circulated even before
        the invasive foreigners arrived
            on their big northward trespass.
Strange people astride big,
        snorting deer-like tame animals.
There were bad jokes
        about unnatural mating and strange anatomy.
We thought the intruders
        might be a different species.
Ones dressed in brown fuss
        over imitations of the four cardinal directions.
But the strangers were actually human,
        albeit deformed, depraved, and stupid,
        with sick skin and too much hair,
            and their stink incredible.
They did not bathe.

They did not speak properly.
     They had no manners.
They were hungry when food was all around.
     We assumed they were not fully evolved.
But the ridicule ceased when we learned
     how efficiently they killed,
          their war dogs, and their deadly diseases.

Amazing stories came from the Red River People,
     where intruders arrived in strange boats
          like Live Things because their wings moved.
Those intruders were different,
     they were friendly and brought gifts.
Later encounters
     down the Gulf were the usual
          roaring and killing like lightning.
Island warriors tied sea turtle bladders
     to their waist-cords, and popped the bladders
          when the foreigners fired.
But the noise wasn't loud enough to kill the intruders.

1750
Panspermia
a hot topic for the next century
popularized in 1974 by Sir Fred Hoyle
     and student Chandra Wickramasinghe.
And discounted by mainstream science.
Space and eternal life,
     traveling between worlds.
Microbial Earth from Mars
     or another star system.
Alien life evolving trillions of species,
maybe we are all Martians.

Behold the Mighty Water Bear.
Tiny tardigrades

World's toughest animals
You see them in water and moist places
Some have sex, most are clones
Soft and plump, less than a millimeter
        waddling on stubby little fat feet
            eating bacteria, plant fluids, nematodes
            rotifers, and smaller bears.
Their own phylum.
Twelve hundred species and more unknown.
New Mexico Gila Forest water bears still unstudied
        you find them to peak elevations.
And to 20,000 feet in the Himalayas
to the sea below 13,000 feet. Tropics to poles.
Little bears curl up and survive
        extremes killing anything else.
Freezing, boiling, years of desiccation
        dying and reviving.
Near absolute zero at minus 459°F to over 300°F,
        radiation one thousand times more lethal
            than for any other animal,
        and the vacuum of space.
Miniature multi-organ creatures more complex
        than primordial life-forming molecules.
The little bears are everywhere.
They like wet moss.
I walk up Railroad Canyon in the Black Range
        before summer rains,
        along an archipelago of drying pools.
One is water brimmed,
        green aquatic mosses
        shimmer in the early morning sun.
I look for all female water bears.
Water striders slide across the surface—
        any creature walking on water deserves respect.
Mosses in the next pool

are exposed and browning,
    and in the next and the next, less and less water
    until the last one is bone dry.
As pool dries, water striders, whirligigs
    and squadrons of water bears
    skip to the next nearest water.
Like the archipelago of Gulf of California desert islands,
    from largest island of highest life diversity
    to smaller and ever more arid ones,
      down to a tiny birdshit island
      with only one plant species.
Is our solar system an archipelago of life
    skipping from a drying dying planet
    to the next best one?
How about archipelagos of solar systems and galaxies,
the ever expanding and shrinking
    Music of the Spheres.
Invaders from another canyon pool,
continent, or galaxy.

1799

Animals are still everywhere,
    always something to hunt and kill.
Live rivers, marshes and springs too.
The Gila runs cottonwood and willow galleries
    all the way to the Red River
      spreading into the Great Delta.
Wide trails follow the rivers like the ones
    along which those southern devils
    led foreign trespassers
    northward into our land.
We swim anywhere and walk in speckle-shaded
    smooth damp trails,
      pungent seep-willow river smells,
      places of no spines.

Our brethren are plentiful, the beavers, otters, ducks,
      herons, cranes, egrets, turtles, and frogs,
         although you shouldn't eat certain ones.
Our rivers run bouquets of fish
      like the Colorado hundred-pound
         six-foot pike-minnow.
River living is easy, although The People
      are everywhere except
         on top of the Big Mountain
            where only the brave go for visions.
Giant Snake lives up there,
      crossing canyons without going to the bottom.
We heard it moving around last night after our hunt.

1845

The Copper Mines, Minas de Cobre de Santa Rita.
Not our name for home place.
We want settlers and miners to go away.
Their diseases kill more than half The People,
      children and elders go first.
After close encounters we fumigate homes and clothing
      with oily smoke from all-thorn wood.
We fight for our land. They call us savages.
Sometimes it seems like the end,
      like Hopi prophesies say
         the end will come
            when strangers
               put a house in the sky.

1940

It's story time.
Elder Old Woman
      relives a childhood trip
crossing the sea on reed balsas tied side by side.
Children are tied to strong men rowing.
That's how we went to the Island of Large Lizards.

Elder Old Man sang to the shore
    and we landed near the rocks.

10,000 years ago and tomorrow
The ancestors made do
    with animals and plants,
        energy no older than decades
        or perhaps a century burning trees.
Clubs, spears and arrows.
When Jesus and Moctezuma conferred
    at the Hill of the Rooster,
        250 million living on earth.
Nothing moved faster than a horse
Population stirring,
    launching boats to catch the wind
        to invade farthest reaches.
Then 400 million
    and we get guns and gunpowder.
Machines invented.
The pace picks up.
Scarfing geologic energy:
    Paleozoic coal and Mesozoic oil
    balance surging populace.
Topping two billion,
    cosmic energy equalizer over
        Hiroshima and Eniwetok.
Electronics quicken
    and all velocities hurry along.
We displace animals,
    and another billion in four years,
        to balance all the animals gone.
Atomics balance the future.

2017
"Curiosity Rover Eats Mars Dirt, Finds Odd Bright Stuff"
Engineers don't have time

to sterilize all the dirt eating drill
        or even Curiosity's exoskeleton.
Probably not much chance to contaminate Mars. Probably not.
Engineers, not biologists
        savvy to invasive species.

2047

GooAp brings precious metal from a nearby planet,
        although they say it's from their asteroid.
Free enterprise thrives on efficiency
stockholders want returns.
Cut costs, cut sterilization.

2049

I don't know how you found out
        because there's nobody left.
A strange microbe rode in
        on that GooAp space train.
Ate all our chlorophyll.
Leaving only water bear
to carry on.

Election Day Promises

Coyote says
spring will last forever
But hummingbird
waves washing over
the garden battle
genetic tides from Mexico
sucking everything red
from the tropics

weaver woman strips long blackdevil's claw bones
sown into the fertile whirlwind
with white seeds
as coyote fills her burden basket
with welfare

mesquite moons
on the canyon rim
saguaros
on the dark side
the condominium
rising to the canyon rim

Coyote gets grants
holds office
calls you to meetings
and puts you on hold
His friends
all live in adobes
restored with passive energy
federal funds

Coyote
promises spring wildflowers
carpeting the desert

Warning to Politicians

Come sit oily on the beach
    come sort your bones
        in the marble museum.

Species yet to evolve will not remember your name.
Daturas and golden agaves and boojums
    in the Viscaino fog will not vote for you.
At dusk old pelicans come home
    and unionized bats skim little poison fish
        off the top of the ocean sea
while the whales and turtles call for each other
    and none answer.

Frost kills the last amaranth
    yellow mustards shed seeds in the drying air.
At last it is time to drink cactus wine
    and streak the earth red for rain.

Hey Pancho Villa
    did you really steal the treasure map
        and cut out their hearts
right there in front of fringe-toed sand lizard?
Don't worry, it will be all right
    we will make you King of Dunes.
You can dine on undescribed pupfish
    and go on to harness solar energy
        and photosynthesize your own
so you won't need our plants and animals.
We'll carry flat-tail horned lizards
    and all knowledge
        into the galaxies
beyond I'itoi.

Cocking the Gun for Gaia

I

If there is adaptive benefit for consciousness
it is to do enough before it is too late
You say it is too late
You are probably right
but we are still here and so are great turtles in the sea

Why is population not in the headlines
Population has not dropped

Population cocks the gun for war
and locks step with weaponry, warfare,
and pandemics
This is the world we make
extinctions, global warming, and despots
while baby turtles paddle across the ocean sea

You say it is a joke
that the way forward would be an addictive
male sterilant pill (reversible)
in the hands of women
Think about it, even if gentler

Territoriality and conflict are in your genes
but you became the mistress of our genes
If we own war, who owns peace

Gaia requires balance, for you and me,
for the universe and for all time
Gaia does not lose. Gaia does not win. Gaia pervades
Gaia balances war, weaponry, and population

We will talk about that later
we will talk about that on the way to our food
Red-head Vulture and Black-head Vulture

they talk about that
they talk about the hunt
they cooperate
one sees and one smells
They talk about that, eating the dead

Population cocks the gun for war
What will the children do

II
Gaia sipped a mint julep
and
floated an angel
upside down
through Doors of No Return

rocket jockeys
ignorant of invasive species warning
bring back extraterrestrial rocks and ore
Gaia resets the Anthropocene

Acknowledgments

The first edition is dedicated to Mahina Drees with gratitude and admiration. Kindred friendships and adventures leading to *Dark Horses* include strong influences from many friends. I especially thank:

John Brandi

Cathy Stackpole Bunnell

Sterling Bunnell

Diane di Prima

Allen Ginsberg

Diana Hadley

Drummond Hadley

Peggy Hitchcock

Joanna McClure

Michael McClure

Gary Nabhan

Betsy Sandlin

Mac (Mary A.) Schweitzer

and so many others.

For writerly encouragement and inspiration for this second edition, I especially acknowledge:

Susan M. Berry

Peter Blystone

Susan Davis Carnahan

Ann Lane Hedlund

Bonnie Maldonado

Jim Malusa

Gregory McNamee

Sharman Apt Russell

James Thomas Verrier

Robert Anthony Villa

Benjamin Theodore Wilder

Robert Hazard Winston

and most especially Silke Schneider

plus everyone else who should be included.

A Note on the Birth of This Book

During the alternative press revolution of the late Sixties and early Seventies the kind of authors I was seeking for Tooth of Time Press stood apart from academic literary types. They were of the category of up-from-under people who could comfortably gather at a table of comrades who shared an overlapping array of interdisciplinary pursuits: poetry, science, botany, medicine, archeology, jazz, opera, oceanography, Zen, modern dance, baseball, auto racing, theater, water divining, piano tuning, etc. Richard Felger—as a scientist, poet, watershed walker, bioregional explorer, student of medicinal plants, rock art, Original peoples, and ancient cultures—was one of those people. Michael McClure was another. One of my many meetings with Michael was at Richard's house in Tucson, coinciding with a visit to a Yaqui Deer Dance ceremony. He greatly admired *Dark Horses and Little Turtles*, acclaiming not only Richard's poems but also his drawings, his "word maps," his visual approach to poetry on the page: topographic-typographic projections of the landscape.

Dark Horses and Little Turtles was one of the very first books I published in a small-press series dedicated to "the exploration/meditation/narration of astral and biogeographical hemispheres." It appeared in 1974 as a Tooth of Time Books limited-edition chapbook: 200 handbound copies printed on a hand-cranked 1909 Rotary Neostyle mimeograph machine (the book and the mimeo are now in the collection of UC Berkeley's Bancroft Library). The desert itself came alive the minute you opened the sand-colored 11 × 8 newsprint cover graced with Richard's calligraphy and turtle-petroglyph line drawings. The 28-page interior contained poems, maps, a play, and fanciful drawings—pollywogs, river ripples, amoebic forms, turtles, bird-turtles, turtle-humanoids—all printed in brown ink. At $2.50 a copy, the book quickly got to old friends, new readers, and future fans. It was a unique experience in publishing that evolved into a lifelong friendship, and it all began with correspondence and travels between my mountain cabin in New Mexico's Sangre de Cristo outback and Richard's corn-planted, lophophora-pollinated home in the Arizona desert. I am glad to see the book resurrected in its present form. ¡Viva!

JOHN BRANDI
Río Arriba, New Mexico

A Note on the Rebirth of This Book

It was fifty years ago that Michael McClure suggested putting together some of my writings. John Brandi published 200 copies on his hand-cranked press.

Robert A. Villa, renowned Sonoran Desert herpetologist and plant expert, found *Dark Horses and Little Turtles* on Mark Dimmitt's bookshelf. Robert said it should be republished and contacted Tucson-based writer and editor Gregory McNamee, who amazed me by offering to republish it. After half a century I made a few revisions and added some new writings.

As curator of botany at the Natural History Museum in Los Angeles, I made a number of trips to work on specimens at the California Academy of Sciences in Golden Gate Park in San Francisco and at the University of California Herbarium in Berkeley. My involvements with population and environment led to friendships with artists and scientists in the Bay Area and beyond. It was heady times and we were protesting war and assaults on nature. John Brandi, Michael McClure, and Allen Ginsberg encouraged me to keep writing, which I did, although my primary focus has been botanical research.

I kept up my botanical and ecological research and writings, and from time to time wrote poetry and other non-peer-review works. Here are two poems from a 2017 reading hosted by Ben Wilder at the Desert Laboratory on Tumamoc Hill, University of Arizona:

> Fitting agriculture
>   to the Land is the easiest
> Your world has 30,000 species
>   of food plants
> Choose yours
>   for food resiliency
> From deserts to tropics
>   to match dreams of the Land

Stand up straight, your posture is bad,
    you are going to grow up crooked.
When you are 6 and 7
    and into marine biology— mostly shells
the good stuff is in the beach drift
so I look down for bio-treasure
    in the dry drift.
Adults don't understand
    and they never will.
I suppose I never will grow up
    at least I can stand up straight.

RICHARD STEPHEN FELGER
Headwaters of the Gila

www.ingramcontent.com/pod-product-compliance
Lightning Source LLC
Chambersburg PA
CBHW080926050426
42334CB00055B/2828